Becoming a Great Sight-Reader –
or *Not!*

Follow my quest for piano sight-reading nirvana, and learn what you should and shouldn't do.

By Al Macy

http://AlMacyStuff.com

Table of Contents

Introduction – How I Got Into This Mess!

December 10, 2007

Today I decided to become a great (or at least, good) piano sight-reader. Although I'm already a jazz piano player, with 4-6 gigs per month, my sight-reading is lousy. Really lousy. I'll bet that most seven-year-olds who have had a year of lessons read music better than I.

I never practice, and I still sight-read better than you!

My plan is to get the best advice on how to improve my sight-reading skills, and then devote 2+ hours per day to sight-reading practice – **for at least one year**.

If you are in the same situation, you may be asking yourself what's required to reach this goal, and how long it will take. You're also scouring the web looking for tips on how to jump-start your sight-reading. Well, I'm writing this for you. OK, also to show how clever I am, but *mostly* for you.

The subtitle of my book talks about my quest for "sight-reading nirvana" because I figured it would look good on the cover, plus it should up my sales with the huge Buddhist piano sight-reading demographic. So, borrowing from the real definition of "nirvana," this is what I'm after:

> A transcendent state in which there is neither suffering, desire, nor sense of self, and the subject can readily play new piano music, as long as it's not too difficult.

Yeah, that's my quest.

IMPORTANT: you may want to read this entire book (or at least skip to the end) before you begin, so that you can benefit from my experiences, and not head down any dead-ends.

Why I Want to be a Good Sight-Reader: I've found that I don't need to be a good sight-reader to play small-combo jazz. Most jazz musicians read from jazz "charts." These consist of single note melodies along with the chords. I don't have much trouble with these charts, since I can read the melody easily, and my left hand knows how to play the chords. However:

- Once in a while I might need to read standard music to play with, for example, a big band.
- I don't feel like I'm a real piano player if I can't read music well.
- I'd be embarrassed if someone said "Hey, Al plays piano, let's have him accompany us with this Christmas carol music!"
- Occasionally I use some educational material (for example, transcriptions, sample intros or endings), and it would be convenient to be able to read it quickly.
- I like the process of acquiring a new skill.

My Musical Background: For you to evaluate whether your experience in learning to sight-read will match mine, you need to know a little about my musical background. So, here's a boring look at my history.

As a young kid I played piano by ear, but never took formal lessons. I had some records with Bach piano pieces on them, played them at 16 RPM (on this thing called a "record player" – playing a 33 RPM record at 16 RPM makes the music slow, and brings it down about an octave), and learned parts of them by ear. This makes me sound more like a prodigy than I was – I only did this for a few pieces, and it took a long time. Eventually my mom took pity on me and bought me the sheet music, and I would laboriously figure out a measure or two, and memorize the piece that way. The main point is that I went out of my way to avoid learning to read music.

At age nine I took up trombone, and studied it seriously until the final year of high school, when a scheduling conflict between chemistry and band made me choose between music and science. I chose science (phew, that was close!).

As required by the 1960s law that stated that every teenager has to play rock and roll guitar, I also took lessons in guitar, and played in a rock band. I even performed in a Simon and Garfunkel type duo, at "The Chicken Coop," once a week, getting paid $2.50 plus one piece of fried chicken.

But I pretty much did nothing with music from college until 1987 (age 34), when my interest in jazz was rekindled by hearing the tune "All of Me" in Steve Martin's movie of the same name.

I took formal piano lessons for a year or two, worked hard, and learned a lot, but the sight-reading just wasn't happening.

In 1992 (age 38) I picked up the trombone again, and got serious about jazz trombone. My sight-reading was better on trombone than piano (hey, only one note at a time!), but I still needed to polish it up for big band playing. I played jazz trombone seriously until 2005 (age 52), performing with a number of large and small groups.

In 2005, I was having some problems with my shoulder, caused by too much trombone playing, so it was time to switch back to piano. This time I concentrated on jazz, and didn't work much on sight-reading. That is, my playing consisted of playing the chord changes, with improvisation in the right hand. That has worked well, and I now lead a jazz quartet (Sax, drums, bass, and piano), and also play in duos (Sax & piano or piano & bass) and trios. To see my music web sites, go to AlMacyStuff.com.

One other thing relevant to sight-reading: I've always been a speedy typist. In college, I had this thing called a "typewriter," which is like a papery laptop. I wanted to cure myself of the bad habit of looking at the keys, so I put tape over the letter names on all of the keys. That solved my problem after only a week. The thing about typing is that there is no conscious thought on my part. I think of a sentence and it magically appears. Wouldn't it be nice if I could get that way with piano?

This last November, I reread the book *A Soprano on her Head*, and it inspired me to give sight-reading another chance.

Yay, that's the end of the long boring history. The main point was that I was pretty musical, but avoided learning to sight-read chordal piano music very well. It may be that my window of opportunity closed when I was a kid.

Now to find out whether I can learn to sight-read!

Readers and Memorizers – Which are You?

December 11, 2007

In *A Soprano on Her Head,* the author notes that there are two kinds of musicians: readers and memorizers.

Readers can sit down and sight-read a new piece well, but wish they were good at memorizing or at playing by ear.

Memorizers, who are often also good at playing by ear, can hardly avoid memorizing a piece of music that they play multiple times, but wish that they could sight-read better.

This makes sense, because if you're a memorizer, you get less sight-reading practice. That is, if you play a piece ten times, you're only sight-reading it once or twice. You may not memorize it completely after one time, but you get some benefit from your memory, and you generally remember what comes next. A reader, however, is (almost) sight-reading it each time, and thus getting 5-10 times more sight-reading practice!

Also, if you play well by ear, you're going to find that if you know the tune, you don't read the melody, and just play it by ear. I remember that once I said "Hey, I'm really getting this sight-reading stuff!" but soon realized that I was playing well because I wasn't reading the melody at all, just playing it by ear.

That's my problem: I'm a memorizer. So, to solve this problem, I'll get my hands on tons of easy piano material so that I never have to play the same piece twice.

Sight-Reading Tips from the Intergoogle

December 14, 2007

[The tips in this chapter are great, but see the "Sh*t My Teacher Says" chapter for some tips that I posted after working on sight-reading for four years.]

I started my sight-reading quest by finding all the web site tips and tricks I could. Here are the tips I like the most (they are described in more detail in the links below):

- Practice playing with your eyes closed (exercises, memorized pieces, etc.). If you never have to look down at the keyboard, sight-reading will be easier. Blind pianists can do it, so can you.
- Play at a steady pace and don't stop to fix mistakes (don't "stutter"). I find this very hard advice to follow.
- Look ahead. This is something else I have trouble with, but I'm working on it.
- Learn to recognize intervals instead of individual notes.

For links to sight-reading tips found on the Internet, please visit AlMacyStuff.com.

Collecting Your Sight-Reading Material

December 15, 2007

If I'm going to sight-read all new pieces, and I'm going to do it two hours per day I'm going to need literally hundreds of easy piano pieces! Here are just some of the books I've collected:

Here's where I got them:

- Online: Google "free easy piano music" and you'll find a number of sites with printable music. Unfortunately, you'll need to download and print each piece individually.
- From a friend who had a lot of sheet music in her closets (Thanks, Dottie!)
- The Brick-and-Mortar Public Library: Yay!! This is the best resource. I've found lots of music at all levels.

- Hymnals: A must have for sight-reading practice. Through PaperBackSwap.com, I got a Christian Science hymnal and a Presbyterian hymnal. The first was printed in 1938 but is in great shape (they don't make books like they used to).

Am I Dyslexic or Something??

December 17,2007

Well, I've been at it for about a week, and I'm starting to wonder if I have some kind of undiagnosed dyslexia! Sometimes I'll read the bass clef as treble, or the bass clef in the right hand, etc.

I'd also like to know what kind of sick, twisted jerk came up with the idea of two clefs which, although they look exactly the same, represent different notes. Perhaps it was just a joke played by a medieval monk.

A large part of my learning effort is devoted to inhibiting the bass clef interpretation of a note so that I can read the correct treble clef value. I've learned both, but since I used bass clef exclusively for seven years as a child (trombone), that's the one that tries to take charge when I'm looking at a note.

There was a famous musician who gave lectures about music to kids. He would start a talk by having a ten-year-old girl come up on the stage, and ask her to rip the Manhattan phone book in half. She couldn't do it, of course, so he'd whisper a few words to her, put her behind a screen, and at the end of the lecture she'd come out with the book in two pieces. She did it by ripping one page at a time.

The point here was that when you have a daunting task ahead of you, it can help to destroy something. Ha ha. No, the point is that if you can accept small increments of progress, you can eventually solve a big problem.

As I'm playing some of these hymns and other songs at a glacial tempo, I just have to have faith that I will eventually get better. Each day I improve by the thickness of a single, thin piece of paper.

While I'm plodding through some of these easy pieces, it doesn't seem possible that anyone could actually sight-read them at a realistic tempo, but I know, of course that it can be done.

Keeping yourself from slowing down or stopping is much more difficult than you might think, even with the metronome running. The best remedy is to play along with others, but I'll have to improve a lot before I can find some way to do that.

Similarly, looking ahead is not working for me at this point. I can sometimes look ahead a measure, but memorizing the next measure while simultaneously playing the current one is not happening.

I have a few things going for me. My hands generally know where the notes are, so I usually don't have to look down from the music. Bigger jumps are a problem, though, so I try to spend some time each day playing jazz, scales, or other exercises blindfolded.

Also, I'm finding that my theory background helps a lot. That is, I know what accidentals to expect, and knowing what chord is likely to come up helps me play it.

Dumb Clefs, Smart Clefs

December 18, 2007

In this post, I'm going to make a simple suggestion that would make piano music much easier to learn, and easier to play. It's probably totally unrealistic, but here we go...

Take a look at this note that you might see written on a page of music:

That symbol represents an "A" if it's on the treble clef, but on the bass clef, it represents a "C". Looks exactly the same, but means different things on different clefs.

Isn't that a strange system? Think of the accidents you'd have if a stop sign meant "Stop" when on the left side of the street, and "One Way" if it were on the right.

So, wouldn't it be nice if the notes were the same on the two clefs?

Here's a suggestion about an alternate version of the bass clef that will result in notes being represented the same way on the two clefs. The change needed to make it this way is a simple one, and it would greatly benefit anyone who has to learn two clefs. Here's a description of the change.

Current System (Dumb Clefs): There are a lot of clefs that are used in writing music, but there are two that are much more common than others: the treble clef and the bass clef. Combined together they are referred to as the grand staff. This is what it looks like (below the keyboard):

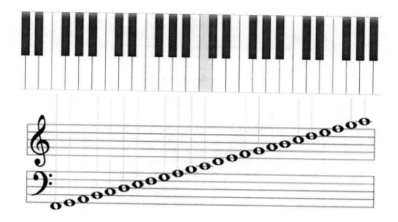

This looks nice and neat, but here's the problem. This arrangement results in different notes being represented by the same written notes on the different staves. As I mentioned above, this representation:

refers to an A if it's on the treble clef, but a C if on the bass clef. Looks exactly the same, means two different things.

Here are the note names on the grand staff:

To learn just the notes shown in this figure, you (or a seven-year-old student) would have to memorize 38 different notes!

But much worse, a single representation of a note, like this,

looks exactly the same to your brain whether you are dealing with treble or bass clef, yet it represents two different notes. No matter how well you know your music, your brain still has to go through that extra step and say "OK, if this were the bass clef that would be a C, but we are dealing with the treble clef here, so that is an A."

There's a surprisingly easy to fix this.

Suggested System (Smart Clefs): Imagine that the grand staff were slightly different, like this:

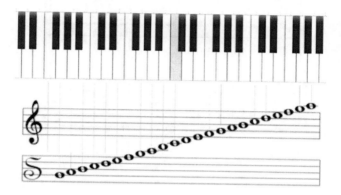

It looks just as nice and neat as the grand staff you're used to, but with a single additional note (two ledger lines total) inserted between the two staves. This simple change gives us a tremendous advantage: The notes are in the same places on each staff!

Note that I've called the lower clef a "Smart clef," and it's represented with an "S". Here are the note names on this new grand staff:

So, for example, this:

represents an A, no matter which clef you are reading from. On the upper staff it's an A above middle C, and on the lower, it's an A about an octave below middle C.

Think about what this change would mean. Students would have their memorizing task cut in half (only about 16 notes instead of 38). They'd learn their notes in half the time.

Better, your brain can process the notes faster when sight-reading (OK, I made this part up, but it makes sense).

If publishers could agree to print beginner piano music (or all music) with these new clefs, a lot of time, effort, and frustration would be saved.

Objections: I've been surprised to find that if I talk about a change like this, I usually hear some (violent) objections. Here's what I've heard:

Objection 1: Once you get used to the standard clefs you won't have problems.

Sure, but it will take you longer to learn them. Also, I suspect that your performance would always be a little better if you can avoid that extra processing step.

Objection 2: There are plenty of staves (tenor, soprano, etc.); treble and bass are just two among many.

True, but they are the ones used by most, and most piano music is written on them.

Objection 3: The current grand staff is symmetrical around middle C, and it makes sense.

The smart clef is also symmetrical and makes just as much sense. It just happens to be symmetrical around a B instead of a C. Some people like the fact that there's only one ledger line between the staves. The new system has two. The two staves are rarely printed so close to one another that there's only room for one ledger line between them anyway. In that regard, the smart clef makes more sense.

Objection 4: You're going to change the piano keyboard??!!

No, no changes to the keyboard or to any instruments are necessary. Someone actually voiced this objection.

Objection 5: I'm already proficient with the current system. I don't want a new clef to learn.

There's nothing new for you to learn. The notes in the smart clef are in the same location as on the treble clef. You can probably adapt to it in a day or so. I know this because often music has sections notated with two treble clefs or two bass clefs. This is especially true of music written for four hands. Those situations are not difficult to deal with.

Objection 6: Nice idea, but most music is already written with the standard grand staff.

Ah, here's a real problem. Literally billions (with a "B") of sheets of music have been printed with the treble and bass clef.

But, look at the state of downloadable sheet music. On some web sites, you can download songs and print them in any key. Digital displays are used in some applications and will be more common in ten years. We are entering a period of transition to a newer way of displaying music, and now might be a good time to make a change.

That's fine, you might say, but let's say a kid who's learned piano using the smart clef system wants to get some music from the library and play it? She will be out of luck!

True, but this situation occurs today, since some older music is written in unfamiliar clefs. When playing trombone, I came across exercises and pieces written for tenor clef, a clef I've never learned.

In rare cases, when the music isn't available in smart clef, and can't be converted, the student will have to learn the bass clef, in which case she will be no worse off than she is today. Better off, since she's already been playing a while, and doesn't have to learn two new clefs at once.

Conclusion: Humans have a surprisingly high tolerance for different standards. Here are some examples:

- Philips head versus Slotted screwdrivers
- Standard time versus Daylight time
- Metric versus English systems
- Democrats versus Republicans
- ePub books versus Kindle books
- PCs versus Macintoshes
- Driving on the left versus Driving on the right
- Calculator keypads versus Telephone keypads (take a look!)

That may explain why people have tolerated the current system for so long.

Yes, it may be unreasonable to suggest a change like this, and I'm sure someone else has already proposed it. At least it's something to think about, and that's why I wrote this chapter.

Finally, Some Progress!

January 19, 2008

Well, it's been about 40 days and 40 nights of two-hour-per-day sight-reading, and I'm starting to see some signs of improvement! Not as much as I'd expect, considering I've now sight-read through *over 700 pieces*, but enough to notice.

I'm noticing, for example, that some of the more common note groupings are quickly recognized and converted into movement of my fingers with less conscious thought on my part. Also, notes which were less familiar before, are now less likely to slow me down. For example, the C two octaves above middle C (two ledger lines above the treble staff) is now more familiar to me, and doesn't throw me off. No more "Whoa – what's that note?"

I'm still playing things at a much slower than normal tempo. For example, I might play a difficult (for me) piece at 60 BPM per eighth note! For most pieces, I set the metronome to 50 BPM (for quarter notes).

To give you a feeling for where I stand, I find that I can sight-read this piece, first time through, quite well at 50 BPM:

Whereas I'll have some trouble sight-reading this piece at the same tempo:

The hymnals have been the most useful, since they have so many chords and intervals to practice.

In addition to these books,

I have read through America's Song Book, Young America's Music, Easy Piano Classics, and about 200 hymns.

I suspect two reasons for my slow progress:

1. At age 54, perhaps I've missed the critical period for learning reading-related skills. Conventional wisdom holds that adults have a much harder time learning to read text than do children. There's some controversy about that, but it may be related to my slow progress. It could also be that I've just had more time to build up bad habits (like attending to notes rather than intervals) than, say, a seven-year-old.

2. Yes, I've read through 700 pieces already but I've only been working at it for one month. If one can become a good sight-reader in ten years by reading 15 minutes per day, it doesn't mean that one can accomplish the same thing in three months by reading 10 hours per day. In other words, there's a passage of time component that's also important in learning a skill like this.

Sight-Singing First: I've done some limited experiments with sight-singing part of a piece first, to see if it will improve my sight-reading. Result: doesn't seem to help. That is, if I sight-sing a line of the melody before playing it, I don't play it any better than I would have without the sight-singing.

Not Looking at my Hands: As mentioned, this is something I'm pretty good at, but I notice that every once in a while I do glance down, and this often causes me to make mistakes.

In addition to playing memorized pieces and jazz with my eyes closed, here's one other exercise I find useful: Close your eyes, place a hand on the keyboard, and try to recognize where it landed by feel. You're not allowed to move the hand; recognize the position based only on the keys you can feel immediately.

Looking Ahead: I realize the importance of this, but I don't do it very well. I have to consciously force myself to do it. It usually goes like this:

1. I think: "Hey, you've got to look ahead more!"
2. I look ahead a measure, and memorize part of it, say the left hand.
3. I play that measure, but I'm so absorbed in playing what I've memorized, that I don't look ahead to the next.

I'm giving this a high priority right now.

Read Intervals, Ignore Notes

January 21, 2008

Today I've noticed that if I consciously try to ignore the individual notes in a two-note chord, and instead look at it as an interval with a given top or bottom note, it makes the reading easier.

For example, instead of seeing this:

as a C and an A (in treble clef), I see it as a sixth, with a C as the lower note.

I knew from the start that that would help, but today found that an "I am NOT going to look at the individual notes!" attitude is helpful.

I'm finding that one key to faster sight-reading, is to have the music trigger movement of my hands rather than result in some kind of intellectual process. As soon as the interval is recognized as a sixth, my hand automatically adjusts itself to the shape needed to play a sixth.

One More Time – Playing a Piece More Than Once

January 22, 2008

Throughout this process I generally limit myself to playing a piece one time only. The idea here is that the second time through it's no longer sight-reading, it's practicing. The thing I want to learn is sight-reading.

On the other hand, I find that I do get some benefits from playing a song a second or even a third time:

- Although I have trouble making myself look ahead while playing, it's much easier the second time through. Hopefully this will give me some much-needed practice in this important skill.
- On the second go-round, I get a chance to see the things that caused problems during sight-reading – things that I ignored the first time. For example, on first reading I might have a problem with a few measures and think "I wonder what went wrong there?" Second time through, I can see "Oh, that was a problem because there's contrary motion in the two hands." or "That was a problem because the notes aren't what you'd expect."

By the way, it's amazing how much easier the pieces are the second time through. I'm not sure what's going on, since I certainly don't memorize the song in one run through. I guess just having a general knowledge of what's going to happen next is enough to improve my playing. Perhaps I should spend a little more time pre-reading the music before I start playing.

Progress Report – After 1.5 Months

January 25, 2008

As an example of my progress, today I sight-read this piece at 55 BPM without making too many mistakes.

Yesterday, however, I played some simpler pieces, and had difficulty – some days forward, some days back. It's always difficult to gauge your progress, since every song is different. You'll start celebrating your success, only to realize that you hadn't improved, the songs were just simpler than the ones you played the day before.

This also happens: I'll be playing some common song, and think "Hey, this is really working, I must be improving!" only to realize that I've been playing the melody by ear, and only reading the bass part – hadn't even glanced at the melody.

Speaking of that, I've found that I can play one hand of a song, even if there are a lot of chords, pretty fast. Not surprising, I guess, since it's only half the music, but it's a good feeling, and I look forward to playing both hands at that speed.

Many people recommend working only with pieces that you can play reasonably well at 50 BPM. I suspect that you can still learn a lot playing a piece that's more difficult, but it's a lot more frustrating. So, if you're worried that you'll give up, go for the easier material.

You really have to be motivated to make this work. If I hadn't decided that I was going to spend a year on this no matter what, I probably would have given up by now. I know this is true, since I've given up on sight-reading twice in the past.

I'm still "into it," and I'm often practicing three hours of sight-reading in a day, but there are some days when I have to force myself through the mandatory two hours.

I'm still finding enough material from the library and from books lent to me by friends, but I've realized that I don't have to have a strict "one song, one time" policy. That is, after I've read through a few hundred songs, I can probably go back and read them again without getting much benefit from my first reading.

One other note: If you're starting out, I'd recommend recording your sight-reading of a few pieces, so that later you'll have a feeling for how much you've improved. Alternatively, you can just make some notes about what songs you played at what tempos.

Looking/Memorizing Ahead

January 25, 2008

The concept of looking ahead as you play is an important one, and I'm working hard on developing this skill. The idea is this: most sight-readers are scanning and memorizing upcoming notes while their hands are on autopilot, playing the current measure with no conscious thought necessary.

In today's chapter I talk about some things I've learned on this topic.

There are a few people who claim that they do not look ahead at all. I know this because I've seen forum threads like this:

Mary: I don't read ahead at all when I sight-reading!

Bob: I'm sure you do, you just don't realize it.

Mary: No, I don't look ahead at all.

Bob: Then you must not be a very good sight-reader.

Mary: Yes I am, I won the New York State sight-reading competition five times.

Bob: You're a liar and you are stupid.

Mary: No, you are stupid.

However, most good sight-readers feel that looking ahead is an important component of their skill.

I used to think that sight-readers looked several measures ahead, but it seems that most only scan ahead about one measure at most.

Here's an exercise that a piano teacher did with me years ago: She let me study a measure as long as I wanted, but when I gave a nod to indicate that I'd memorized it, she'd cover it up. I wasn't allowed to play it until it was covered. This would continue with each measure of the song. The idea was that I'd play one measure while memorizing the next – just as I should be doing when sight-reading.

I hated that exercise! Yesterday I tried doing it myself, forcing myself not to look at a measure while playing it, and I still hate it. I think I know why I don't like it. Take a look at this line from a song I used for this exercise:

This is a very simple piece, but there's a lot going on in some of those measures! Take the first measure, for example, how are you going to memorize that quickly? It's much easier just to play it. Can you do this in two seconds (the time allotted to one measure at 120 BPM)?

"OK, let's see. First beat, there's a B in the bass with a minor third starting on D in the right hand, then both hands play a G, followed by a D in the bass, with a B and an F in the right hand, BTW all quarter notes so far, and now the last beat has another G in the bass and treble, but the right hand G is a dotted eighth followed by a sixteenth."

Or perhaps, in a more sophisticated way:

"OK, the bass arpeggiates a half-diminished B minor with 1-5-3-5 quarter notes, while the right hand first does the 3-5 of the chord, up an octave, plus the sixth, then a 1-5, followed by a pair of G eighth notes that are swung."

Even those long descriptions don't adequately describe the measure.

Presumably I would be memorizing that measure in a more non-verbal way, perhaps even memorizing the way my hands would feel as it's played. Maybe I'll be able to do that in the future, but for now, this is just too much stuff for me to memorize; it's more information than humans can normally put in their short term memory.

So yesterday I had this revelation:

I don't have to look/memorize ahead a whole measure at a time.

The distance ahead that I scan can depend on the difficulty or simplicity of the measures. When there's a lot of information in the notes, I might read only the next beat as I play the current one. When I come to a measure that's simple, I can take the time to look further ahead.

Now that I'm no longer rigidly trying to bite off full measures at a time, I've had more success looking ahead. Yes there are still times when the current notes are difficult enough for me that all looking ahead gets canceled until further notice, but for very simple music I can experience the concept of looking/memorizing ahead first hand, and it feels good.

What a Pain – When (Ouch) Pain Interferes

January 29, 2008

Looks like something is different when I'm sight-reading than when playing my normal jazz, since I'm starting to get a real pain in the back. That is, years of several hours/day with no pain, and now, pain.

To find out what's different, I did some sight-reading, then played some jazz. I noticed immediately that I'm a lot more relaxed when playing jazz. Posture is about the same, but when sight-reading, I'm holding my torso in position rather than just relaxing.

Today I was able to go about an hour with no pain, due either to consciously relaxing, or the three ibuprofens that I took. I'll have to space out my sight-reading practice in order to get at least two hours in every day.

I've dealt with repetitive strain injuries before, and I expect I can lick this.

It's the Intervals, Stupid

January 29, 2008

As mentioned before, quick recognition of intervals seems like one of the keys to sight-reading well. That is, I expect my sight-reading to be faster and easier if I can learn to see this

as a sixth with E as the lower note (bass clef) rather than as an E and a C. Why do I think that? Well, first, as soon as I know I'm dealing with, for example, a sixth, my fingers automatically take on the proper positioning for playing a sixth. Second, when I try to force myself to use intervals, sight-reading seems a little easier.

One problem is that, for the larger intervals, and to my untrained eye, it's hard to quickly see what interval I'm dealing with. For example, the difference between a sixth and a seventh is hard to see in an instant.

I figured I need to learn to "attend to the distinctive features" of the different intervals, as one of my psych professors would say. So here's something I've tried – no idea whether it's useful or not.

I sit down with a piece of music and scan along one clef as quickly as possible and call out the different intervals.

For example, for this music:

I'd say "5, 3, 1, 6, 8, 6, 5, 5, 6, 8, 8, 9," etc.

Will this help? Who knows?

One Hand at a Time – Divide and Conquer

January 30, 2008

In an online discussion of sight-reading tips, one piano teacher recommended reading through an entire hymnal playing only the left hand part, then going through a second time playing the right hand, and finally playing both parts.

So for the last two days I've been playing just the left hand part of the hymns, and this exercise has some advantages:

- First, I'm playing at speed (for example 85 BPM). This gives me practice at recognizing and playing intervals *quickly*. If I want to learn to play pieces at the normal tempo, perhaps it's smart to do some practicing at a normal tempo.
- Second, I have a little more time for working on looking ahead, and recognizing intervals. Yes, I'm playing faster, but it feels that my mind is freed up a little to work on these aspects of sight-reading.
- Third, one gets more playing in. I can plow through almost twice as many songs when I'm playing this fast.
- Fourth, it's less discouraging. When playing things at a glacial pace, they don't even sound like music. Even if it's just the bass part, it sounds more musical when playing at a more normal tempo.

However, this exercise has one big disadvantage: I'm not practicing the one thing that gives me the most difficulty, namely reading and playing four or more notes in two hands at the same time.

So, I plan to use this learning technique in addition to my hands-together practicing. In just the two days I've been doing this, I already feel that my left hand playing is more automatic, with less conscious thought required. Some passages just seem to play themselves.

On a side note, one problem with hymns is that they'll often include intervals in the left hand that are not playable with one hand. Like this:

This is a bother, since you have to interrupt your sight-reading practice to deal with it. Some piano forum members recommend either playing the upper note with the right hand, moving the lower note up and octave, or playing the lower note and a copy of it up an octave.

Progress Report – 2 Months

February 10, 2008

I'm now one sixth of the way through the year, and where do I stand? Well, progress continues, but it is still less than I had hoped for.

Some days I'll have a breakthrough, but it's always hard to tell whether I've gotten better or just hit a patch of easier songs.

For example, a few days ago I'd already put in my hours of practice, and was surfing the web for some new sight-reading tips. After looking through KeyPiano.com, and some other sites, I realized that though I've been working at recognizing intervals rather than pairs of notes, I should extend this concept further. That is, I should try to see all the music in terms of intervals. For example, instead of seeing this (treble clef):

as a a sixth with B in the bottom, followed by a third with E in the bottom, followed by a D, I should see it like this: A sixth with B in the bottom, then move up a fourth, and play a third, then move down one step.

The idea is to eliminate all note names as much as possible, and just look at the movements within the notes in the key.

I tried this out, and immediately saw an improvement! However, the next day my new skill wasn't as evident.

So I continue to slog along. I've read through an entire Presbyterian hymnal – some of it reading only one hand at a time.

My middle back pain has gotten worse, so now it hurts on jazz gigs as well as during sight-reading practice. I'll be on a surfing trip in a month or so, so perhaps it will heal given a break in practicing. Until then, ibuprofen is my friend.

Progress Report – 3 Months

March 12, 2008

Here's the short summary of this month: I'm still making progress, but I lost one week to the pain in the back, and one week to a surfing vacation in Hawaii.

Pain in the Back – Solved? The practicing-related pain in the back continued to get worse. Some of my jazz gigs were torture. Assuming that the basic cause is bad posture, I worked on several ways of solving it.

First was to make a wedge, to put on the piano bench, that would tilt my torso forward, and force me to sit up straight.

That didn't really do it, since I could still sit in such a way that allowed me to slouch.

I then tried putting together my piano bench such that it was tilted, and putting it end-on to the piano.

This was just too uncomfortable.

Finally, I found a solution: Use a chair.

I was surprised to find that my computer chair, at full height, was the same height as my piano bench. If I sit with my back supported by the back of the chair, the pain is much less. I had one three hour piano gig with no pain at all.

[A note from the future, January 4, 2014: I'm back to playing on a regular piano bench, many hours per day, with no pain. I do use a small wedge cushion to help me with my posture. The improvement may be simply due to the passage of time (aches and pains come and go), but I've also eliminated crunches from my exercise routine, and do planks instead. I also do more stretching, upper body strength training, and the "shoulder-blade squeeze" exercise.]

I expect this will solve my problem. Another thing that should help is a week away from the piano. I implemented this cure by flying to Hawaii with my wife for a week of surfing, hiking, and drinking.

We returned yesterday, so it's now back to work with two hours per day of sight-reading!

Progress Report with Recordings

March 24, 2008

I continue to make slow but steady progress. While I see a real difference in how well I sight-read, I'm still surprised that I haven't progressed further.

I wish I had some revolutionary insights to pass along to others suffering along this path. I will say that to some extent, all that matters is doing it. That is, I've talked a lot about things like recognizing intervals, but if you do enough sight-reading, that's going to happen whether you try to force it or not [A note from the future, January 6, 2014: I no longer think this is true. Later chapters will discuss this].

One article I saw said that an important component of learning sight-reading involved learning hundreds of common patterns. That's happening for me. That is, I'll see some common pattern and be able to play it instantly. I can take in larger blocks of notes at once. There's an indescribable change in how I see the music.

Unfortunately, I find that even when playing the simplest of music, I can still have a problem reading some part of it. And I am still not good at playing anything fast.

I'm hoping that I'm going to progress more quickly now – as if what I've learned so far will let me gain traction, and move faster. My #1 short-term goal is to get better at looking ahead in the music.

Samples of My Playing: Well, I've put this off long enough – it's time to let you hear some of my sight-reading (oh, man, do I have to?). Embarrassing, but this is the best way to show what 3.5 months of heavy-duty sight-reading has bought me.

To hear me play these samples, use the web browser on your computer to go to AlMacyStuff.com, and click on the link that says "Click Here for Internet Links for *Becoming a Great Sight Reader -- or Not!*" If you have any trouble with that, please drop me an email at FoggyBeach@gmail.com.

The first sample is of the song "On a Slow Boat to China." Here's the music – not terribly challenging, but not super easy either.

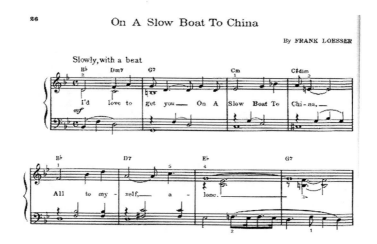

Go to AlMacyStuff.com to listen to me sight-reading this for the first time. Pitiful, huh? You can hear how slowly I have to play it. But at least I was good about not going back and correcting mistakes, right? I also noticed, in listening to it and reading along, that I'm playing some parts the way that I remember the tune, rather than playing exactly what's written.

Go to AlMacyStuff.com to hear how I sound after I've read it through 5-10 times. In this recording, after I read through this first page, I start playing as if it were a lead sheet. That is, I ignore what's written, play the chord in the left hand, and play the melody in the right.

Next is a hymn from my 1937 Christian Science Hymnal, which I picked up for free from www.PaperBackSwap.com:

Based on my handling of measure 2, I'm probably not going to heaven, but go to AlMacyStuff.com to listen to me play this with a church organ sound.

Now, here's an early classical piece:

Rondino

Go to AlMacyStuff.com to hear it sight-read. Beautiful, huh? Sign me up for Carnegie hall. I have the most trouble with music that has separate musical lines going on at once. And for those of you who noticed that I didn't follow the dynamics, phrase markings, or staccato notations, two words: bite me!

And I'll finish off with three sophisticated melodies, "Humpty Dumpty," "Goosey Goosey Gander," and "Tom Tom the Piper's Son." These are from *It's Easy to Play Nursery Rhymes*, which actually has good arrangements with some surprisingly nice chord voicings.

Go to AlMacyStuff.com to listen to me knock Humpty Dumpty off his wall.

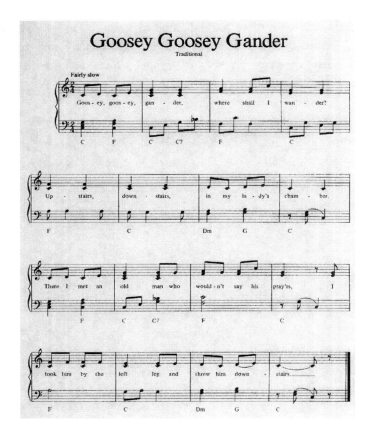

Go to AlMacyStuff.com to bring Goosey Goosey to life.

Go to AlMacyStuff.com for my tasteful rendition of Tom Tom.

So ends my recital. Hopefully, when I'm done with my year of sight-reading, I will be able to sight-read pieces like these at a normal tempo. We'll see.

Hit the Accelerator – Playing Faster, Sometimes

April 5, 2008

Well, things are starting to happen. Today I got a book out from the library that I had borrowed back in December, and pieces that I could barely get through at 50 BPM I can now read at 80-102 BPM. What's better is that I have a feeling that the music just flows out.

The music is very easy, but hopefully this is a sign of things to come.

Hitting the Accelerator: Prompted by a post by Akira in a piano forum, I realized that instead of choosing a tempo at which I make only a few mistakes, perhaps I should speed things up a bit. That is, play at a speed at which I make lots of mistakes. This seems to be a good thing.

For the last few days I've been choosing tempos that are fast enough that I can just barely keep track of all the notes. Above this tempo, I start to ignore parts of the music (usually the left hand); at this tempo, I feel like I'm just holding on by my fingertips.

This works well because it forces me to interpret the notes quickly, and move my hands quickly.

A lot of people suggest that your sight-reading will improve rapidly if you play a lot of duets with others. If practical (it's not practical for me), this is a good idea since it forces you not to stop and go back and correct your mistakes. But I'll bet that another reason this is good is that you probably play things faster than you would if you were practicing alone.

I'll let you know whether this new paradigm works for me.

Hymnal on Steroids: Yesterday I received a copy of Bach's 371 Harmonized Chorales and 69 Chorale Melodies, which was recommended on a forum. But found that it's like hymns on steroids, and is too difficult for me now. The print is very small, too.

Progress – New Recordings

April 22, 2008

Not much new to report. I have been faithfully doing at least two hours of sight-reading each morning. I have good days and bad. I recorded the same songs that I presented in an earlier chapter and I'm encouraged that I've improved a bit more than I had realized. You can visit that chapter to see the sheet music for these recordings.

Of course, it's not technically sight-reading to play these pieces again, but it's been a while since I played them, so you can still make a comparison. For the Rondino, I had a technical problem when recording, so I had to record it again, so that one had a little more practice this time around.

Use your computer's browser to go to AlMacyStuff.com and listen to the recordings of my playing then and now.

Halfway There – Six Months Hard Labor

June 10, 2008

It's now been six months since I started my piano sight-reading; I'm halfway towards my goal of two hours per day for one year.

I know it doesn't make sense, but I'm both amazed at how far I've progressed, and disappointed that I haven't gotten further. Some apparently simple songs give me a lot of difficulty, however, it's exciting to be able to read pieces which I know would have been impossible for me to play six months ago.

I've settled into the following routine: I start sight-reading early in the morning (7 or 8 AM – I'm a morning person) and read one hour of hymns followed by an hour of other music. I've read through both hymnals twice. If I'm not having a good day, I'll allow myself to skip anything with four or more sharps. I prefer the flat keys – perhaps because of my trombone background. I especially like Eb.

I'll set the metronome somewhere between 50 BPM for a hard hymn, and 80 for an easy one. If I like a hymn, I'll repeat it a few times at faster and faster tempos. Sometimes I'm surprised to find that it's not that much more difficult at a faster pace.

For popular music, such as this:

I usually play without the metronome, but will soon be using the metronome at 50 BPM.

Here's an interesting phenomenon that I've noticed: sometimes I can be reading a song (a hymn for example), start thinking about something else, and find that I'm still playing. I'm neither better nor worse when this happens, but my mind is elsewhere, and I'm sight-reading on autopilot. I don't know if this is good or bad, but it is interesting.

Ask some expert sight-readers what they're doing when sight-reading, and sometimes they'll say "I don't know – it just happens." I'm hoping that this book is valuable because I'm reporting what I find as I learn. Perhaps I can report what's happening for me before I cross over to the other side. Here are some insights:

It's *Not* the Intervals, Stupid! In earlier chapters I spent a lot of time talking about recognizing intervals instead of individual notes. Well, I now think that may be a waste of time. As you get better, you are recognizing patterns of notes, and it doesn't matter whether you try to recognize intervals or not. It's just going to happen, if you practice enough, that you recognize patterns. [Note from the future, January 4, 2014: As you see, I've gone back and forth on this. However, I now believe that it is the intervals. That is, seeing intervals rather than notes is important.]

I'm getting into the "I don't know — it just happens" zone, but let me try to explain with an example. Here's the start of a hymn from an earlier chapter that is quite easy for me to play:

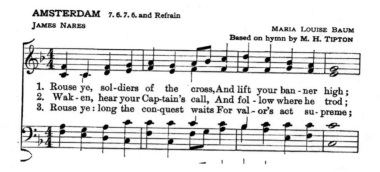

When I see this, the notes in the first measure are seen as "F chord, C chord, Dm chord, C chord." Or maybe I'd say that my mind is saying "Oh yeah, there's that common F chord pattern with 1 and 3 in the bass, and 5 and 1 in the right hand, etc." I'm not always thinking in terms of chords, but there's often some thought about how the notes make sense.

Those patterns of notes come up so frequently, that it's just a "recognize it and play it" situation. I don't know if this is good or bad, but it is what is happening for me. As soon as a hymn gets out of the typical range of notes, it's harder to play, because the patterns aren't as familiar. Same thing for less-common key signatures.

Thinking about intervals does help whenever I see a pattern such as this:

At which point I don't think about individual notes, just think about "moving the interval around" in the current scale.

Again, it may be bad advice to say that you don't need to pay attention to intervals – I'm just relating what has been happening with me.

Looking Ahead: I still feel that I'm not looking ahead enough. I am still forcing myself to do it, at least when I think of it, and hope that at some point it will become automatic. This doesn't seem to be something that will just happen as I keep playing.

Once in a while I do pretty well at looking ahead, and it feels good. There's a kind of rapid "look here, look there, up there, down there" feeling that seems to be effective. Like a little bird flitting around. I rarely am looking forward more than a half measure or so, unless the current measure is very easy. What often happens is this: I decide that I'm really going to concentrate on looking ahead for this piece. I do pretty well until a difficult measure comes up. Then I get stuck figuring out the notes I'm playing, and after that have a difficult time getting ahead again.

I still do less well when skipping to a new line – not sure what that means.

Good Days and Bad Days: I continue to see this: one day I feel like I'm doing great, and really getting the hang of this sight-reading thing, and then the next day I'm amazed at how bad I am. You might think "Oh, you just happen to play more difficult pieces on a bad day." However, recently I made a list of hymns that were quite easy for me to play. On a bad day, I tried those, and didn't do so well.

Playing without the metronome usually makes me feel that I'm doing better – guess I must be slowing down at the more difficult places.

I'll be Twice as Good: If I'm twice as good at sight-reading on Dec 10, 2008 as I am today, I'll be satisfied.

Still Working Away

August 19, 2008

I haven't given up – I'm still working at it. I've had to take a few days off here and there when I had important gigs coming up, and needed to work on some pieces. Also, I have to admit that there are some days when I only work for an hour instead of two. I've found that it's easiest on my back if I don't work two hours in a row, and sometimes I don't get back to the piano for that second hour.

I've cut down on my jazz gigs until December so I'll have more time for sight-reading.

I generally do an hour of hymns (I'm coming up on five times through both hymnals) plus an hour of popular or traditional music.

I'm still happy about what I've learned but disappointed that I haven't learned more. This is one of the hardest things I've done.

I've also noticed an improvement of my single line + chord jazz sight-reading, which is nice.

Practice Session Recorded – Ten Minutes in the Life...

September 4, 2008

Here's a sample of what it sounds like when I practice sight-reading. This recording is the first ten minutes of my hymnal sight-reading practice today. I start with Hymn #288 in the Presbyterian hymnal, and continue through the book from there.

Go to AlMacyStuff.com to listen to this recording.

I've mentioned how some days seem better and some worse. This one was closer to the "worse" side. It will be a bit painful to listen to at times, but I'd say it gives a fair indication of where I stand right now.

I Did It!

December 9, 2008

Today I fulfilled my vow to practice sight-reading for two hours a day for an entire year! Of course there were some days that I missed, and some days when I practiced less than two hours, but I'm sure I put in at least 650 hours of sight-reading. I read through two hymnals seven times each!

How did it turn out? Well, I didn't progress nearly as far as I had expected to. For example, I thought that after that much practicing I would be able to play any hymn at any reasonable speed. Instead I can play easier hymns at about 85-100 BPM, and most hymns at 60 BPM. I thought I'd be able to rocket through any "Easy Piano" piece, and play most pop or jazz music without too much trouble, but that is not the case.

If someone were to say "Hey, Al plays piano, let's have him accompany us with this Christmas carol music!" could I do it? Maybe. If the music weren't too difficult, if the singers weren't too discriminating, or if I had a chance to run through them a few times, then the answer is yes. Otherwise the results would be sketchy. Here's what you might expect: these are two Christmas songs that I've played multiple times, but have not memorized:

Go to AlMacyStuff.com to hear these recordings.

So, while I'm disappointed that I didn't reach those goals, I am pleased to have made solid progress. I am no longer a sight-reading dimwit. Sometimes I can read through a new piece well, and get a feeling for what it would be like to be a great sight-reader.

Below I'll give advice to others who are just starting out and talk about where I go from here, but first let's look objectively at how far I've come.

Progress Recordings: As I've gone along, I've periodically recorded a small number of songs to track my progress. Of course, each time I play one of these benchmarks, I learn it a bit. However, playing them a few times over the course of a year doesn't make that much difference. I've played one of these (hymn 296) about seven times (once each time I went through the hymnal), but I don't think that has made a big difference.

I regret that I didn't record my playing when I started out. The first progress recordings were made after I'd been working on sight-reading for 3.5 months. Anyway, here they are.

(Go to AlMacyStuff.com to hear these recordings.)

On that web site, you can also listen to "Another Hymn" that I hadn't recorded previously. Although on a better day I might have done better, these two hymn recordings give a good indication of where I stand after one year of sight-reading.

Although I never recorded it before, I had noted in an early chapter that after 1.5 months I could play this song:

at 55 BPM without too many mistakes. Go to AlMacyStuff.com to hear it sight-read today (1 year) at 80 BPM.

Surprisingly, some of these didn't improve much between 4.5 months and one year. Perhaps I just wasn't playing well today. Another possibility is that I played too many hymns and not enough other types of music, resulting in less progress with those types. Note that after playing Slow Boat two more times, it sounded a lot better (Go to AlMacyStuff.com to hear it). This represents a benefit of my improved sight-reading – it makes it faster to practice something. I can read through it multiple times in much less time.

Note also that I was more nervous than usual – I knew that I had only one chance to play it right, and that whatever I recorded would be published here on the Internet.

Advice to Others Seeking To Improve Their Sight-Reading Quickly

- If you're like me, **it's going to be a lot more difficult than you expect**. I thought that after a month or two, I'd start to gain traction, and progress rapidly from that point. Instead it's been a slow, steady slog all year long. Maybe you will learn faster. I generally learn things pretty quickly, especially if I put in a lot of effort, but on the other hand, I am over 50 years old, and may have missed the critical period for learning to sight-read. If you're like me, you will need a lot of willpower.
- **Record yourself extensively on day one**. I waited 3.5 months before recording myself, mainly because I didn't want any record of

how atrocious my sight-reading was. Now I wish I could compare today's playing with that of a year ago.

- If you can afford the wait, I expect that **you'll do better with four years of 30 minutes per day than with one year of 2 hours per day**. I don't have any evidence for this, but I suspect that that's why my 650+ hours of sight-reading didn't pay off as well as expected.

- Remember in my earlier chapters I talked about seeing intervals versus notes, things like that? Well forget it, that's all BS. **You just sight-read a lot and you'll improve.** I'm not seeing intervals, I just see the music on the page and am increasingly able to quickly convert that into movements of my hands and fingers. [January 4, 2014: I now believe: (1) Intervals *are* important, and (2) "just sight-reading a lot" is *not* enough to improve quickly.]

- **Sight-Read the type of music you want to play.** I worked on hymns over 50% of the time even though that's not my goal. Hymns are the most comfortable thing to play and quite enjoyable. Each one is short, you know what to expect, the harmonies sound great, and most notes fall within a set range. But unless you want to be a church organist, be sure to include a lot of other types of music as well. The samples above show how I improved more for hymns than for other types of music.

- Finally, I still feel that **looking ahead is an important aspect of good sight-reading**. The better you get, the easier that is, but I still have to remind myself to consciously look ahead. When I do that, it seems to help.

Where Do I Go From Here? I'm hooked on sight-reading, and still want to be good at it. My plan now is to practice sight-reading at least 30 minutes per day (instead of two hours). I can see the light at the end of the tunnel, so I'm not going to quit now. I plan to meet my original goals by this time next year.

Progress Report – 1.25 Years

March 23, 2009

Since finishing the year of sight-reading, I've continued reading at least 30 minutes a day, sometimes significantly more. I'm reading only modern/pop/standards stuff – no hymns or classical.

I'm quite pleased with my recent progress. It feels like things are finally coming together. As a side benefit, I'm noticing more confidence in my jazz reading (that is, reading melody lines while playing chords). I'm also finding that working with transcriptions or educational piano stuff like this

is a lot more convenient, since I can play the examples much faster.

As an example of my progress, today I sight-read this piece pretty well (but with a lot of mistakes) at about 50 BPM:

I'm realizing that much of my progress is based on a new-found quick, involuntary understanding of the notes on the page. That is, I see, I understand, I play. To show you what I mean, look at the following sentence, but don't read or understand it:

I went to the store.

I'll bet that there isn't one person among you who could look at that sentence without reading it and understanding what it meant. That's what I'm now getting with the music. I see the notes and instantly have a feeling for what they mean and how I'd move my hands to play them. I also realize that this is something that takes time to develop.

Shorter Practice Time: Here's a comment concerning 30 minutes versus two hours per day: One benefit to the shorter time is that perhaps I do less practicing of bad habits. For example, it's hard to force myself to look ahead all the time when playing for two hours. As a result, I'm doing a lot of practicing of sight-reading without looking ahead. When practicing for a shorter time, I can focus more on practicing the good habits.

Things I am continually working on that seem to help:
- Focus on reading ahead
- Make sure I don't look down at my hands at all
- Feel the keys
- Always play with the metronome

So now I'm just continuing to sight-read, attempting to gradually increase the tempo at which I play songs.

Progress Report – 1.75 Years

September 15, 2009

Things are still coming together, but more slowly than expected. I see the end of the tunnel, but I figure it's about two years away. That is, I expect that in another two years, I'll be a really good sight-reader.

Before continuing, let me show you where I stand. Here is a piece I sight-read:

Go to AlMacyStuff.com to hear me sight-read Wabash Cannonball and When My Sugar Walks Down the Street.

So, I'm getting the hang of things, but I'm still quite slow. I just can't keep up if I increase the tempo. (I realize that got some of the rhythms wrong on the latter song.)

Not Looking at my Hands: One thing that I'm really, really good at is not looking at my hands. I can read an entire song, and not even glance down once, even when there are big jumps. I highly recommend getting this ability nailed. It feels really cool, and I never have to worry about losing my place in the music.

There are two things going on here: Feeling the keys, and knowing where they are.

Concerning feeling the keys, you have to get into the habit of caressing them all the time. Imagine that you are a lovesick teenager, and the keys are your girlfriend. You just can't get enough of touching her/them.

As for knowing where they are, I should give some credit to the book *Super Sight Reading Secrets* by Howard Richman. His keyboard orientation drills made me realize that I could move my finger to a note pretty accurately with my eyes closed, even if I wasn't starting from a known note. Here's the exercise I do:

I make sure I am sitting right in front of middle D (that is, with my belly button lined up with the middle of the middle D key). Then I close my eyes, put my hands in my lap, then think of a note and move a finger to it. I found that often I get the note exactly right, and my accuracy improves with this drill. In other words, the feeling of where your arm is can be pretty good for hitting the note you want.

Combined with feeling the keys, this ability can help you eliminate your need to look at the keys. It's true that finding a note is a lot easier one note at a time, with no time constraint, than it is when in the middle of some complex song. Also, I sometimes get "desynchronized" with the keys, and play, for example, an E when I'm expecting a B (that is, I'm at the top of two black keys (E) when I think my finger is at the top of three black keys (B). But once you get some ability and confidence here, you might find that you can make those big skips without thinking about them.

I'm hoping that the habit of not looking down at my hands will get so ingrained in me, that I won't do it even if I'm playing in public or am nervous.

As an aside, musicians often wonder why they can play something perfectly at home, but have big problems with the same piece when they are performing in front of someone. One reason is that when nervous, you do things differently. For example, you may look at your hands because you are worried that you will hit the wrong note. No wonder all hell breaks loose. I've found that the best cure for this is to play in front of people as much as possible.

Looking Ahead: Looking ahead as I'm playing is still a struggle for me, and I continue to work on it. I play better when I do it, but that just may mean that the song is easier, and it gives me a chance to look ahead. That is, I look ahead because the song is easy, the song isn't easy because I look ahead.

Sometimes I try to look ahead just a half measure or so. I played prelude one in Bach's Well-Tempered Clavier yesterday, and was able to zip through it with almost no errors. Why? Because each measure repeats the same five notes twice, so there's plenty of time to read and understand the next measure as I'm playing the current one. If I can just get that same idea working for other songs, I'll be set.

That's it for now, sight-reading fans.

Two Years and Counting

December 10, 2009

Well, I've now been working on my sight-reading for two years! Where does the time go, huh? I'm continuing to improve, and more importantly, I'm reaping the benefits of my new skill:

- It's great to be able to read and play examples in instructional jazz texts.

- I'm enjoying learning pieces by reading through them multiple times. For example, go to AlMacyStuff.com to hear me play this nice arrangement of "Have Yourself a Merry Little Christmas" (from the *Reader's Digest book of Christmas Songs*).

- I'm finding that it's much easier to memorize songs when I can read pretty well. Instead of laboriously reading through a measure or two at a time, I can more quickly play a segment of the song and commit it to memory. For example, I've recently memorized Bach's Two-Part Invention #8, Bach's French Suite 5 Allemande, and Schubert's Scenes from Childhood (Foreign Lands & People).

Back to the actual sight-reading progress aspect, I've continued to do about an hour of reading per day. I do more repeated readings of songs – while technically not sight-reading, this has the benefit of letting me practice reading at a higher tempo.

I'm getting more comfortable at sight-reading. That is, it's less of a strain than it was in the past. Things are becoming more automatic, and my hands go where they are supposed to go with less conscious thought.

As mentioned before, I'm good at not looking at my hands, but I could still be much better at reading ahead. Here are several examples of my sight-reading, recorded yesterday. They give a pretty good feeling for where I stand, although I play better when I'm not making a recording destined for the *world wide* web.

Go to AlMacyStuff.com to listen to the recordings.

That's it for now. I'm continuing to work on this, and I'll report back in a year!

Getting Professional Help

January 15, 2011

It's been over a year since my last chapter; now three years from the start of my quest.

During this last year, I haven't done quite as much sight-reading as I did during the first two years, since I've had a lot of gigs and have been working on other piano tasks. I've done a good bit more non-sight reading, that is, reading the same piece repeatedly to get better at it instead of memorizing it. I have even performed a simple piece from music – a first for me.

I've continued improving, but way too slowly.

But today, I took my first lesson with an accomplished teacher who is confident that she can help me improve faster! This is big news.

During the lesson she had me sight-read a very simple classical piece. I did a great job at demonstrating how poorly I sight-read. I was hampered a bit because I forgot to bring my piano glasses, and by performance anxiety, but in general I think I communicated my level of skill in this area.

Some of her initial comments were:

- I should spend *much* more time analyzing the piece before I play it, checking all the way through for what will be happening, noticing patterns, thinking about the key, etc.
- Intervals are indeed important, and I have to get better at thinking about intervals instead of individual notes. I should be thinking more of relationships between notes. One exercise is to say the interval out loud ("second," "third," "fifth," etc.) either while playing or away from the piano.
- I need to always practice not stopping or slowing down; I should make rhythm the first priority.
- It's best to start at a slow tempo, and work my way up.
- I should think more about where I'm looking. Not only looking ahead, but also making sure I scan up and down, and not get locked into just the treble or bass clef.
- I should pay attention to the fingering suggestions, seeing them as something that will help me.

Let me tell you what a big deal this is. I am very much a "work on my own" guy – a typical INTJ introvert. That's what kept me from seeking help long ago. In fact, on the way to my first lesson, I decided that I definitely would not continue with the lessons. But the teacher was so good, that I knew continuing would be a good idea.

I asked her whether I could really become a good sight-reader, and she said "Absolutely!" She didn't actually say "Abso-f**king-lutely," but that's the way she said it, and I could tell that that is what she was thinking.

Another reason this is significant is that I'm a tightwad. The only reason that I'm retired and thus able to spend hours a day at the piano is that I've squirreled away most of my money from an early age. So, to spend $1,300 a year ($50 every other week) on lessons is a big deal for me.

I'm optimistic that this is going to help, and I will keep you posted!

Interesting Observations from Books

March 1, 2011

I've read a lot of books on piano, some good, some less good. Some I liked were *Note by Note, I Really Should be Practicing, Never Too Late, The Piano Shop on the Left Bank,* and *The Inner Game of Music.* But here are two observations that are relevant to my quest for sight-reading nirvana.

In *Note by Note,* the author describes her years of giving piano lessons. One adult student was rich, and really wanted to learn piano fast. So he hired her to give him a six-hour lesson every day. Can you imagine that? The most interesting thing about that, was that the student didn't progress any faster than students who had the normal one hour per week. It suggests that practicing sight-reading two hours per day is not four times as good as doing it 30 minutes per day.

The book *Never too Late,* was written by a man who took up the cello in his late fifties. He wanted to make the point that you can indeed teach old dogs new tricks. He said:

> If I could learn to play the cello well, as I thought I could, I could show by my own example that we all have greater powers than we think; that whatever we want to learn or learn to do, we probably can learn; that our lives and our possibilities are not determined and fixed by what happened to us when we were

little.

However, when I read the book, I was struck by how he had trouble getting good at the cello. If I remember correctly, he ends by saying that he wasn't that good, but that he was steadily improving, and would be much better later. However, in researching him a bit, I found that he died a few years after writing the book. Sorry to sound crass, but it was indeed too late for him (boy, am I going to go to hell when I die!).

Sh*t My Teacher Says

December 6, 2011

My teacher's tips are excellent, but I couldn't resist naming this chapter like the popular book, *Sh*t My Dad Says*.

In a few days I'll be posting my four-year progress report (OMG), but I wanted to get these great tips out to you first.

Here's *my* big tip: You will make much faster progress if you work with a teacher who is very good at teaching sight-reading. This advice is coming from someone (me) who is very independent, and usually likes to work on his own. I've been taking lessons (twice a month) with a Dr. Robin Miller for almost a year now, and I think I've progressed as much in that year than in the three prior years.

Warning 1: There are teachers out there who are not very good at sight-reading. I called one teacher and told her what I wanted, and she told me, actually whispering, "Well, I have to admit that I'm not a very good sight-reader myself."

Warning 2: Even if the teacher is good at sight-reading, he/she may not be able to teach it well. I took a year of lessons in the eighties, but my teacher at the time didn't help my sight-reading much.

I'll tell you about my new teacher, Dr. Robin Miller. She is on the faculty at Humboldt State University, and she's been teaching piano for over 35 years. She can sight-read effortlessly, but more importantly, she sees what I'm doing wrong, and has a bag of tricks and exercises to help me fix my problems. I'll show you what I mean below. I have a lesson every other week, at $50/lesson. Of course it's unlikely that you live close enough for lessons from her, but for completeness, here is her contact information:

- Faculty Web Page: www.humboldt.edu/music/node/376
- Email: rashamelamed@gmail.com
- Phone: (707) 826-5448

Here are some of the tips she has given me. In many cases, I knew these things, but wasn't applying them well.

Tip #1: Intervals are Indeed Important

Robin showed me that I need to pay more attention to intervals. "Hey, Al," you say. "You knew that four years ago!" True, but although I talked and thought about it, I was really still paying attention primarily to the notes. It's frustrating that I was aware of this important key to good sight-reading, but wasn't really employing it well.

Robin has an exercise in which I say the interval by which the melody changes with each note as I play a tune. For example, in this piece:

I would say, out loud, while playing, "Same, second, second, second, fifth, sixth, same, second" etc. Of course you can do the same thing for the bassline, some middle part, or chords. I'm not very good at talking while playing, but this helps me pay attention to the intervals.

I also created some interval flashcards. It may seem elementary, but they help me recognize the intervals very quickly. I use them on my iPod Touch, and I can just scroll quickly from one to another, and call out the interval. You can download all the flashcards from my web page, www.AlMacyStuff.com. They look like this:

So, if you scrolled through those, you'd say "Sixth! Third! Octave!" Realizing that for seconds, fourths, sixths, etc. (that is even intervals) one note is on a line, and the other on a space, helps. This exercise is only difficult when distinguishing the wider intervals (sixths, sevenths, and so on).

One other trick that I developed on my own to help see intervals is to transpose the piece to another key. For example, I might play the above piece in F instead of C. I figure out what the first notes are, and from then on, I must pay attention only to intervals, because the notes will be wrong. For example, in the above song, I'd start with G and F in the left hand, and B natural and F in the right. On beat three I'd move the bass up a half step, and the melody down a second (a minor second in this case).

This transposing is extremely slow, and often I have to go back to the beginning, and start over. But it's very useful, because you are *forced* to ignore the notes.

Back to non-transposing playing, here's an example of how I put all this into practice. Take this hymn:

296

AMSTERDAM 7. 6. 7. 6. and Refrain

JAMES NARES

MARIA LOUISE BAUM
Based on hymn by M. H. TIPTON

1. Rouse ye, sol-diers of the cross, And lift your ban-ner high;
2. Wak-en, hear your Cap-tain's call, And fol-low where he trod;
3. Rouse ye: long the con-quest waits For val-or's act su-preme;

Serv-ants of a might-y cause, Put sloth and slum-ber by.
Rout the cring-ing host of fear By faith that walks with God.
Rouse ye, rest not, do the deeds That break the earth-ly dream.

REFRAIN

Rouse ye, rouse ye, face the foe, Rise to con-quer death and sin;

On with Christ to vic-tory go, O side with God, and win!

Words Copyright, 1932, by THE CHRISTIAN SCIENCE BOARD OF DIRECTORS

Starting with the second measure, my fingers would be on F and C in the left hand, and F and A in the right. For the next chord, in the right hand, I see that I will still have a third between the notes, and I will shift this pair of notes down by a second. In the left hand, I see that the top note, C, is the same, but that the interval for these two notes is now an octave. So I leave my left thumb on C, and shift my hand position to that of an octave, which I know well.

I usually pick the note in each hand that moves the least, move to it, based on the interval of the change, then use the interval between the notes to find the other note.

Now, having said this, do I always pay attention to the intervals and not the notes? No. There are two reasons.

First, after years of thinking about the notes, it's hard to get away from that. Although I've benefited from my years of daily sight-reading, these years of doing it the wrong way have hurt me in this way.

Second, as Robin has pointed out, there are other ways of looking at the music, or taking in the information while sight-reading. One of those ways is the notes themselves (another is the harmonic structure, which I will discuss below).

However, I've felt that paying more attention to intervals has helped me more than any other tip. If I practice for too long, I find myself getting away from intervals. Often it helps to play a piece very slowly, and force myself to consciously think in the way I described in the above hymn example, explicitly thinking "OK, that note goes up a second, and the other note is a sixth below it." Also, if it's too much to do this for all the notes, I might just concentrate on using the intervals in the bass clef, and not thinking about how I play the top notes.

Tip #2: Don't do a Reset with Each Chord

This is an example of how having a teacher can be better than doing it yourself. One day, Robin said, "Let me show you something. This is how *you* play this hymn." and she played it, imitating my style. "Now, this is how *I* play it." and she played it her way.

There was an "Aha!" moment, because I could see immediately that when playing like me, she was essentially removing her fingers from the keys, then "starting over" and finding and playing the next notes. When she played her way, there was this beautiful seamless flow from one chord to the next. That is, it was about moving the fingers in an efficient way from one set of notes to the next. It was partly an issue of fingering, but more an issue of using the changes of the notes rather than the new notes themselves to play the next chord.

Tip #3: Keep the Beat Going

This is the tip that Robin feels is most important. Of course I have always known this, but she has made me work on it more.

Tip #4: Know What to Leave Out

If you keep the beat going, but are having trouble, you can't slow down. So instead, you have to leave something out. Dr. Miller explained that the melody has the first priority, and the lowest note is a close second. That is, you can leave out the middle notes if you need to.

I pretty much knew that, but here's an exercise that helps me "cheat" when I get into trouble. Playing a hymn, Robin would have me play just the outer voices, or just the inner voices, or some other combination. At first this was extremely and embarrassingly difficult. I would have thought that leaving things out would be easy, but I had been seeing the music as a unit. I found that doing this exercise helped me to leave out some notes when necessary. Sometimes I'll practice by playing all four voices, then leaving out one or two for a few measures.

Robin has also noted that I tend to leave out the bass when I get into trouble, getting caught up in the top voices – I need to work on that.

Tip #5: See the Harmonic Structure

The number of chords used in a piece are usually pretty limited, and often predictable, especially in hymns. For example, you can be pretty sure that the second-to-the last chord will be the dominant seventh for the key.

Robin's tip is to get used to instantly knowing what chord is represented by the notes. The exercise she suggests is to say the name of each chord as you play it. So, for example, for the first line of this hymn,

296

AMSTERDAM   7. 6. 7. 6. and Refrain

JAMES NARES

MARIA LOUISE BAUM
Based on hymn by M. H. TIPTON

1. Rouse ye, sol-diers of the   cross, And lift your ban - ner high;
2. Wak - en, hear your Cap-tain's call, And fol - low where he   trod;
3. Rouse ye: long the con-quest waits For val - or's act   su - preme;

Serv-ants of   a might-y   cause, Put sloth and slum-ber by.
Rout the cring-ing host of   fear   By faith that walks with God.
Rouse ye, rest not, do the   deeds That break the earth-ly dream.

REFRAIN

Rouse ye, rouse ye, face   the   foe,   Rise to   con-quer death and sin;

On with Christ to vic -tory go,   O   side with God, and   win!

you'd say: F, C, Dm, C, F, C, F, **C7**, F, Bb, F, C7, F, C. That bolded C7 might just be some passing tones, but it seems to work like a C7. Some tunes are not as easy as that one, with, for example, the tonics of some chords left out, but the basic idea is the same.

I've been a little resistant to this tip. My reasoning is that it seems that you are using the notes to figure out what the chord is, in order to know what the notes are. But you started with the notes, so what's the point?

But apparently the point is to instantly notice the chord, helping you to know ahead of time what the notes will be. I'm going along with this, and it does seem to help. I find that with the common keys I already recognize many of the chords.

One thing I did to gain awareness of the harmonic structure of music was to dissect the chords in a few Bach chorales, and then write my own using those same chords. Here's an example of one.

Chorale 2

It was an interesting exercise, but I'm not sure how much it helped my sight-reading.

Tip #6: Take a Minute to Look Through a Piece Before Playing It

This should perhaps be tip #1, because it's one of the first things my teacher told me. I knew I should be doing this, but felt that it may help my playing, but wouldn't help my sight-reading. In other words, I wanted to practice being surprised by the notes, and dealing with it. But I'm a dutiful student, and I now take the time to check through, looking for clef changes, checking out the rhythmic structure, watching for difficult places, etc. I don't do it as much with hymns, since they are quite predictable, and I enjoy going from one to next, and noticing the sound of the change in key. But this is definitely good advice.

BTW, I don't want to imply that I'm playing only hymns – I also work with modern stuff and non-hymn easy classical pieces.

Tip #7: Shoulda, Woulda, Coulda

At one point early in my lessons I told Robin, "Oh, if only my parents had made me take formal piano lessons when I was in elementary school, I would probably be a good sight-reader now." Her three word reply, put things in perspective. She said, "Oh, shoulda, woulda, coulda." OK, that's four words, but it made me realize that my "if only" attitude wasn't helping. In other words, "Oh, get over it!" She also made me realize that I might not have developed the jazz playing had I had a more standard piano education.

That said, I still fantasize about going back in time and whispering in my parents' ears when they are sleeping: "Make Al take piano lessons at age four. Make Al take piano lessons at age four."

Tip #8: Don't Overdo the Hymns

I was getting better at hymns, but at one point, Robin said "No more hymns!" She explained that hymns have a very limited range (since they are written for voice), and are restricted in their rhythmic variety. Thus, I could get very good at playing hymns, but still have problems with other types of music.

Tip #9: It's OK to Glance at your Hands

This is another tip that I've been resistant to. Robin explained that you should practice glancing down at your hands and back up to the music without losing your place. She said that later on you can play without looking at all, but for now, this is an important skill to have.

I'll stop here and pass on some more tips in future chapters.

In three days it will be **four years** since I started this crusade, and I'll post a progress report along with recordings.

Progress Report – 4 Years!

December 10, 2011

Whoa -- I've been working on this for four years! Hard to believe.

I've worked pretty hard on sight-reading during this last year, mainly because I've been taking lessons. In the last six months in particular, I've felt like I'm finally gaining traction, and seeing a faster rate of improvement. Check out the Sh*t My Teacher Says chapter for a description of what I've been working on, and advice about what has helped my playing the most.

Here are some recordings to give you a feeling of where I stand today.

I've been using the first tunes below for all my progress recordings, so of course it's not strictly sight-reading anymore. Also, I've read through my hymnals many times, so although I don't remember the tunes, I have played them before.

296

AMSTERDAM   7. 6. 7. 6. and Refrain

JAMES NARES

MARIA LOUISE BAUM
Based on hymn by M. H. TIPTON

1. Rouse ye, sol-diers of the cross, And lift your ban - ner high;
2. Wak - en, hear your Cap-tain's call, And fol - low where he trod;
3. Rouse ye: long the con-quest waits For val - or's act su - preme;

Serv-ants of a might-y cause, Put sloth and slum-ber by.
Rout the cring-ing host of fear By faith that walks with God.
Rouse ye, rest not, do the deeds That break the earth-ly dream.

REFRAIN

Rouse ye, rouse ye, face the foe, Rise to con-quer death and sin;

On with Christ to vic-tory go, O side with God, and win!

Words Copyright, 1932, by THE CHRISTIAN SCIENCE BOARD OF DIRECTORS

Go to AlMacyStuff.com to hear how I played this hymn after three months and now.

Go to AlMacyStuff.com to hear me play Humpty Dumpty after three months and now.

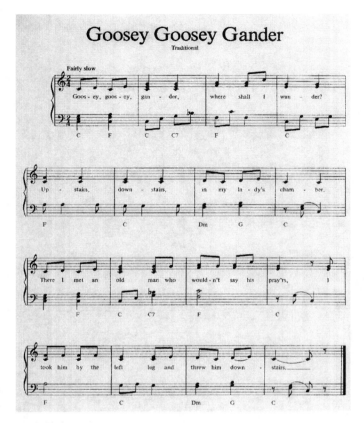

Go to AlMacyStuff.com to hear me play Goosey Goosey after three months and now.

Here is a hymn from a Methodist hymnal that I just got from the library. I have never played it before, but it's possible that the same song is in the other hymnals I've worked with.

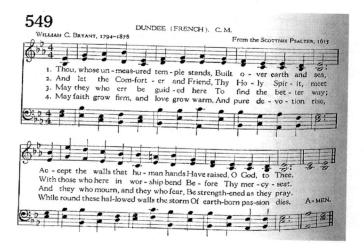

Go to AlMacyStuff.com to hear me play this hymn.

Here is a non-hymn tune from a library book. I've never played this, nor do I recognize the tune.

Go to AlMacyStuff.com to hear me play it.(by the way, I'm aware of the rhythmic errors I made).

Finally, I've mentioned that one of the benefits of my sight-reading work is that I can practice tunes and get better at them without actual memorization. I read through this song a bunch of times each year, though I've never worked on getting it close to perfection.

Go to AlMacyStuff.com to hear me play this tune, and hear my regula playing in one of my Christmas Videos.

That's it for now. I'm hoping that I'll make faster progress this next year – see you then!

Still Plodding Along

August 29, 2012

Just a quick chapter to let you know that I'm still working away, and still doing 1-2 hours of sight-reading every day. The three latest insights from my teacher that have helped recently are (I'll post more about these when I am less busy):

- Leave stuff out. At one of my lessons, my teacher said "I sit here thinking how much better he'd play if only he'd leave things out." That made an impression on me, so now, if I'm playing a hymn or chorale, and I start to have problems, I leave out the middle voices. That is, first priority is the top voice, second is the lowest, and after that, the middle voices. I can now play the Bach chorales (slowly), that were way too difficult when I first encountered them. This works for modern pieces also. Surprisingly, it takes practice to not play each note. When you consciously omit some notes, you get better at it.
- Play slowly. I've known this from the start, but had found that if my metronome was slower than about 50 BPM, it was hard to follow it. Now, I use the metronome beats for eighth notes. For example, for a Bach chorale, I might set it to 60 BPM.
- Learn and see the harmonic structure of a piece. That is, try to understand what chord notes make, and how that chord functions. For example, "These notes make up a G7." I never thought this would help. "What, I see the notes and figure out what chord it is, to understand the notes? How would that help, since I already know what the notes are?" Well, it does seem to help, partly because I

know what notes to expect next. For example, in the last measure of a Bach chorale, I know there's going to be some kind of standard cadence (for example, in the key of C, I might expect an F chord, a G7 chord, and finally a C chord). Even if I don't get all the notes, I can fake it. But it also seems to help me put my fingers down in the right places.

Hang in there fellow sufferers – more later.

Progress Report – Five Long Years!

December 10, 2012

Oh, man, five years gone, and I'm still not that good a sight-reader. Much better than before, but I have a long way to go. There are days that I want to give up on this, but I keep working at it.

I've been doing some reading every day, except that I took about a month off leading up to a solo gig that I had in early December. That is, during that time I put all my effort into working on tunes for that gig, and did no sight-reading. That month saw some good improvement in my solo work, and showed me that my time spent on sight-reading is time taken away from other aspects of my playing. That is, it reminded me that there is a cost for working so hard on sight-reading.

That gig is over, I'm back to daily sight-reading, and I'm trying something new. I've concluded that one of my problems is that I pay too much attention to the note names and not to the intervals. I've discussed this several times before. Because I've spent years not attending to the intervals, my brain has gotten stuck reading notes. This is a case where I've been practicing the wrong thing.

My best trick for fixing this is to transpose a tune to another key (see the "Month of Intervals" chapter). When I do that, I have to pay attention to intervals, because the notes are wrong.

In the past, I've used transposing in this way: I'll play a hymn or two transposed, and then I'll go back to normal reading. After I do that, I seem to pay attention to intervals a little more, but soon go back to my old bad habits.

So my new system is to, each day, play two hymns or chorales transposed, and **then not do any more sight-reading.** Perhaps if I do that for a month, I can kick my mind into the interval gear.

Note that when transposing, I think about intervals only. I'm not allowed to see the note and figure out what note I'll play. I only do that for the first chord of the piece. From then on, I play based on the intervals from one chord to the next. I don't want to get good at transposing, I just want to use transposing as a tool to help me attend to intervals.

A Month of Intervals Only

February 4, 2013

Here's a report on a trick I've used that helps me pay attention to intervals.

After years of paying attention to the notes and not the intervals, I needed a way to break myself of this habit. In other words, when I look at something like this in the treble clef:

I must force myself to see it as a sixth with C as the lower note (or as a sixth with A as the upper note), instead of a C and an A. You may say, "But, Al, what's the difference? C and sixth or C and A – you still have two things to notice." But there are three advantages.

First Advantage: My "muscle memory" knows what a sixth feels like. That is, my hands can form a sixth without much conscious thought. So, instead of seeking out a C and an A, my hand just forms the right interval, and all I need to do is put it in the right place.

Second Advantage: As I go from one note or chord to the next, using the intervals can be more efficient. For example, for the first two chords here (treble clef):

thinking in intervals is more efficient. For the second chord, instead of thinking "find an E and a G" I can think "keep the top note the same as the last chord, and form a third."

Third Advantage: When the music has switched clef, or has a lot of ledger lines to deal with, thinking in intervals will work better. I am so used to having the lower clef be the bass clef, that when it's not, I have to actively inhibit the note names that come to my head as I play. And when I've got a bunch of ledger lines involved, I don't have time to count them. When using intervals, both of these problems magically disappear.

So, assuming that it's best to notice intervals, how do you learn to do it? For me, I could tell myself "Notice the Intervals, Stupid!" but I'd still tend to think about the individual notes. My teacher would have me say the intervals as I played, "Sixth! Third! Fifth!" but I would still predominantly attend to the notes. This didn't really work. That is, I'd know what a sixth or a seventh looked like, but I didn't have that instant recognition.

I needed a magic wand that would make me forget the note names, so I would have to use intervals. I sometimes wished that I were starting over, didn't know the note names, thus learning intervals.

That wand doesn't exist, but I came up with something almost as good.

It's a trick that makes the notes **wrong**, so that I'm forced to use only intervals.

The trick is to transpose! If I play a piece in a different key than the one in which it's written, the notes are wrong, but the intervals are right. Perfect!

For example, let's say that I play this:

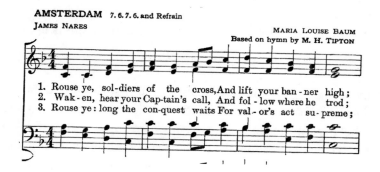

but instead of playing it as written, I play it in the key of C. I will be forced to use intervals only, because all the notes are wrong!

Technically, I do it like this: The first chord has the root as the bottom note and also the top note (F). In the key of C, those notes are C instead of F. In the left hand, I form a third with my fingers to play a C and an E. In the right hand, I form a fourth, playing a G and a C.

Going to the second chord, I notice that in the left hand I'm just going to move that third down one step (a second), and in the right, I'm just going to repeat the lower note.

From the second chord to the third, I notice that in the left hand, the lower note goes down by a second, and I form a fifth with my fingers. In the right hand, the lower note goes up a step, and I form a third. And so on through the entire hymn.

I've dabbled with this trick off and on, but because I went back to regular old reading, the use of intervals never stuck. So I decided that for one month, I would only play transposed music. That is, no notes, only intervals for a month.

I set three rules:

1. I played at least two hymns per day (I made it easier on myself by working with hymns – the main purpose here is to notice intervals, and for this, hymns should work as well as other types of music). A big advantage of hymns is that when you play a wrong note it is immediately apparent.

2. I only allowed myself to read notes for the first chord of a line, unless I got into trouble three times. Since each chord depends on the one before it, once you made a mistake, it's hard to recover. I didn't allow myself to recover by reading the notes. Instead, I made myself go back to the beginning of the line and start again. But if I screwed up three times, I allowed myself to cheat until the next line.

3. I allowed myself to play in "easy" keys, since the benefit of the exercise is independent of key. So I usually transposed to C, and if a hymn was in C, I'd transpose to F.

Did It Work? Yes. Was it a miracle cure? No, but I am now better at attending to intervals rather than notes. In other words, I can more quickly "see" a sixth than I could before. I find myself using intervals even when not transposing.

I found that the technique works best when there is one note in a hand that moves less than a fourth. That's usually the case (as it is in all of the chords in the above example). When transposing, I ended up with a system in which I moved a finger to whichever note moved the least, then formed the interval to get the other note. For example, for the left hand in the above example, going from the third chord to the fourth, I would move the lower finger down a second, then form an octave with my fingers.

Note that I got better at playing transposed. It's still a struggle, but my improvement proves that I am faster at seeing intervals. Also, by not going back to regular playing each day, I never erased the gains that I made.

I currently see it like this: working with intervals is another tool in my toolbox. Sometimes it will help my sight-reading, and other times I will use other tools. For example, when thirds move in stepwise motion, as in chords 3-7 in the treble clef of the above example, thinking of intervals is absolutely the way to go. In other instances, it might help more to think of the harmonic structure or notice the notes themselves.

The bigger the interval, the more problematic it is. For example, in the fourth chord of the above example, left hand, I might think "That's an octave. Or is it? Let's check, C, C, OK, it's an octave." So I still have work to do.

I still need to remember to use this tool. For example, when under the gun, playing something for my teacher, I'm less likely to use intervals.

I plan to use a refresher course of this, and do another month of intervals-only training again.

Or Not!

December 10, 2013

Well, I am done spending one or more hours per day on sight-reading. This is the "-- or Not" section of the "*Becoming a Great Sight-Reader – or Not!*" book. I've spent six years working hard on sight-reading, and I have *not* become a great sight-reader.

I initially called this chapter "I Give Up!" In a way I am giving up, but, on the other hand, I have improved my sight-reading significantly. I've decided that my brain is just not wired for sight-reading, and pursuing this any longer is not a good use of my time.

A better "spin" might be "I've improved my sight-reading enough, and now I'm going to move on to other things." But after six years of concerted effort, I am only a mediocre sight-reader.

I'm quite sure that I did everything right. I practiced diligently for thousands of hours (literally) and I worked with an excellent teacher, but it just didn't happen. It is pretty disappointing, because I had really looked forward to being a good reader, and a good all-round pianist. On the other hand, I am pretty happy with my jazz playing, and the extra time I have to devote to jazz tasks (e.g. new licks, memorizing more tunes, working on my sound, transposing, transcribing, listening, technique, etc.) is already paying off.

I still practice jazz and technique several hours per day, I'm just not devoting much time to practicing sight-reading. Perhaps I will add back some dedicated sight-reading practice, but right now I'm taking a break

As I write this chapter, I'm reminded of how much I want to be a good sight-reader. Perhaps I will continue working on it. However, I've learned that "Just do 15 minutes a day, and you are bound to improve quickly," is not necessarily true for me. One thing I might do is just work on modern tunes rather than on classical pieces, for which I have less use.

Sight-Reading Dos and Don'ts

January 4, 2014

On the title page, I suggested that you "Follow my quest for sight-reading nirvana, and learn what you should and shouldn't do." So, even though I never reached sight-reading nirvana, here are some sight-reading dos and don'ts that I've discovered:

- Do hire a teacher who is good at sight-reading, and good at teaching. If I'd done that on my first day, I think I would have doubled my first year progress (woulda, shoulda, coulda, huh?).
- Don't assume that if you just sight-read a lot, you will get better. This may be true for some people, but you'll probably get better faster if you practice the right way.
- Do learn to pay attention to intervals rather than notes. It's easier said than done, but worth the effort.
- Don't look at your hands.
- Do endeavor to look ahead as you read.
- Don't try to look way ahead – a note or two ahead may be all you need.
- Do be annoyed that the positions on the treble and bass clef represent different notes, but deal with it because it's not going to change.
- Do play at a steady pace and don't stop to fix mistakes. Playing along with someone else is a great way to force you to keep going.
- Do practice playing with your eyes closed. It's challenging and fun, and helps you find keys without looking.
- Do read through hymnals, but realize that you also need to practice

with other types of music.

- Don't assume that one two-hour session of sight-reading is as good as four half-hour sessions.
- Do make a recording of your sight-reading when you start out so that you will be able hear your progress as you go along.
- Do leave stuff out. That is, instead of slowing down, leave out some harmony notes, for example. This is a skill that should be practiced.
- Do enjoy your playing rather than just seeing it as a means to an end.

Loose Ends

In proofreading this manuscript, I've noticed four important topics that I left out: musicality, rhythm, dynamic markings, and fingerings.

Sounding Musical: When I listen to my progress recordings, I notice how unmusical (robotic?) they sound. I was working so hard on playing the right notes, that I forgot to make it sound good. Don't do that (hard advice to follow)!

I also remember playing a tune for some friends at a piano party, playing the the first chorus by reading the music, and then playing the next as I do a jazz tune. At the end, they all immediately said that I sounded too stiff and mechanical for the first chorus.

Rhythm: If you are very good at interpreting the rhythmic information in the music, it will help your sight-reading. If you have to, for example, think about how that triplet will sound, your reading is going to suffer. If this is a problem for you, I recommend the book *Modern Reading Text in 4/4 For All Instruments* by the famous jazz drummer, Louis Bellson. Sit down and sing the rhythms in that book.

Dynamics: I always give this the lowest priority when sight-reading, much to the chagrin of my teacher. If the tune isn't too hard, then I incorporate dynamic markings. Perhaps I shouldn't do it that way, but that's what I do.

Fingering: My teacher explained that the fingerings are there to help me, so I should pay attention to them. I countered that if Donald Trump were whispering stock tips in my ear while I was playing, it would also be to help me, but I've already got enough things to think about. Once in a while I'll notice a fingering, but sheesh, leave me alone, I'm busy!

Conclusion

I've written this book mainly for adult pianists who would like to improve their sight-reading skills. Here's the conclusion from my six years of dedicated sight-reading practice.

> **If you're like me**, you can improve a lot, but you may never reach sight-reading nirvana.

Boy, what a Debbie-Downer! By nirvana, I mean that state in which you can sit down and play a relatively difficult piece that you've never seen before. By relatively difficult, I mean something like a prelude or fugue from Bach's well-tempered clavier, or a Christmas song, or any of the pieces in the *Easy Classics to Moderns* books.

The professional accompanist for my wife's community choir, can play many, many complicated pieces, and they all sound great. My quest has taught me that although I'm generally very good at learning things, this is something I will never be able to do.

The most important part of that conclusion is the phrase "If you're like me." I'm sure that many of you will have less trouble than I did, and will make large gains in just a few months.

And, I'm not saying that if you think you're like me you should give up. I am saying that you shouldn't have unrealistic goals, and you shouldn't be discouraged if your progress is slow.

I hope that this doesn't sound too negative. I'm really glad of the progress that I've made. And, actually, writing this book has made me want to work some more on sight-reading. I think I'll go back to spending 15-30 minutes per day sight-reading, and concentrate on the kind of music I'm most likely to need to play. And maybe a few hymns.

Now I need a drink, and a phone book to destroy!

If you got something out of this book, please give me a six-star rating. Or five-stars, or whatever.

And watch for my next book, *Becoming a Sex God – or Not!*

About the Author

Al Macy lives in far northern California, and isn't actually cross-eyed.

Acknowledgments

Thanks to my wife, Lena, who is an excellent proofreader, despite being Swedish. She is helping with the research for my next book.

Thanks to clker.com and hasslefreeclipart.com for some of the images in this book.

CPSIA information can be obtained at www.ICGtesting.com
Printed in the USA
LVOW06s1224050915

452967LV00031B/1021/P